I love you,
I love you not,
I love you,
Maybe.

# I love you,
# I love you not,
# I love you,
# Maybe.

*Faceless, so little to judge.*

## Brandy Smith

authorHOUSE®

AuthorHouse™
1663 Liberty Drive
Bloomington, IN 47403
www.authorhouse.com
Phone: 1-800-839-8640

First published by AuthorHouse    12/28/2011

ISBN: 978-1-4685-3471-9 (sc)
ISBN: 978-1-4685-3470-2 (ebk)

Library of Congress Control Number: 2011963428

Printed in the United States of America

Any people depicted in stock imagery provided by Thinkstock are models,
and such images are being used for illustrative purposes only.
Certain stock imagery © Thinkstock.

This book is printed on acid-free paper.

# Table of Contents

# Acknowledgments

In no particular order, many thanks . . .

To God, my indescribable, beyond amazing, redeemer. Nothing is possible without You. Nothing is impossible with You.

To Carmen Dahl, for being the first to believe in my words, the first to make *me* believe.

To Kathy Gillispie, for her incredible enthusiasm, always lending an ear I could talk off, and constant reminder of how God is there.

To Kelly Hart and Sarah Clark, for endless editing, high hopes, and love.

To my brilliant mother, for being a tough critic yet still able to find the time to inspire and challenge me.

To the gentlemen whom some of these poems were about, I am a stronger person because of you.

To everyone at AuthorHouse, whose hard work and advice made this possible.

And lastly to you, the reader, you are not alone.

To all the guys who chase girls around the playground,
Held hands in front of friends,
And whispered sweet nothings in awaiting ears.
To all the girls who have been lied to,
Cheated on,
And heart-broken.
To all, who loved and let go.
This is for you.
Never give up.

# Sorrow

"Now I know I have a heart because I can feel it breaking."

—The Wizard of Oz

Realization hit me
All my efforts were in vain,
I'm still loving you forever
But loving you is driving me insane.

So many sleepless nights
Running from goodbyes,
I wonder if you'll miss me
Lord knows I tried.

Knowing you gave up
Is like a blow to the heart,
Making it hard to get up and fight
When all I want to do is hide in the dark.

I can't seem to get up
I just keep getting dragged down,
I feel so alone and unheard; like
I'm screaming my lungs out but no one's around.

I take a look
Disappointed in what I've become,
I wish I could get the urge to fight
But I just feel cold and numb.

Nothing but silence fills the air
My pleads go unanswered
Help just isn't there.

*I love you, I love you not, I love you, Maybe.*
*Brandy Smith*

Cry me a river
Full of your tears,
Tell me something
I want to hear,
Show me you love me
With all of your heart,
Kiss me with the intent
To never stop,
Remember the way
You used to feel for me,
Remember I told you
We were meant to be.

*I love you, I love you not, I love you, Maybe.*
Brandy Smith

I know you never know this
But I see you all the time,
Maybe not in person
But I see you in my mind.

I know you never think about
The things I never say,
I feel like I'm invisible
So I turn and walk away.

So when that day comes
That you finally see,
Just how truly special
You have always been to me.

You will say you love me
I'll look at you with pain,
I'll quickly say I'm sorry
Then turn and walk away.

We are finished
I made it so,
But I still love you
I just hope you know.

I miss the way you made me laugh
But hate how you made me cry,
I did it because of you
Why did you have to lie?

We were so good together
Couldn't you see?
Why did I fall so hard for you?
Why didn't you fall for me?

My world may be crashing down
But when you look at me
My heart races
And I'm spell-bound.

With just one kiss
You make everything fade away,
I can't stop smiling
These feelings are getting harder to convey.

I'm head over heels
So in love with you,
I'm praying you feel the same
Hoping you're in love with me too.

Falling was beyond my control
Maybe it was fate,
The way I lose my breath
The way I can't think straight.

I'm going to make you feel my heart
Maybe even drive you insane,
But I'll always be here
To help you through all the pain.

I'll be you one and only
As long as you are mine,
I can be your everything
If you just give me the time.

Look deep inside
I know you feel it too,
Listen to your heart
It will speak to you.

Take my heart in your hands
Tell me just how you feel,
We will prove everyone wrong
& show them our love is real.

Is it hard for you to breathe?
Are you falling in love with me?
Here is your moment
What will you answer be?

Can you read my heart?
Can you see that deep inside,
Look beyond the transgressions
Then maybe you can really decide.

Can you see past the wounds
That aren't yet gone,
Will you be the one to stay
Or the one to run out on.

Can you see the shame
Written plainly on my face,
Can you choose weather to fight
Or assume I'm not worth the chase.

Will you prove all others wrong
Or just turn and leave,
Can you show me the definition of forever
And make me truly believe.

Can you show me the way love is supposed to be
With the truth I simply can't deny,
Will you stand above the deception, destruction, and lies
Confirming love does exist or allow it to end with a simple
goodbye.

How can you honestly stand there
And act like you're okay?
Where did you find the courage
To let me hurt you this way?

Why can't you be open
And tell me what's on your mind?
How much can you heart take
When I leave you behind?

Who gave you a heart of gold
To love me like you do?
Oh when will you just understand
We'll never make it through?

I don't think you get it
I just don't feel the same
When will you stop waiting
For my mind to change?

Don't just say I'm beautiful
Don't just say I'm smart,
I want you to really mean it
From the bottom of your heart.

Don't bother to try and help me
I'm sure you won't even care,
Just take all your stupid lies
And get them out of here.

Don't call me just to talk
And end with an "I love you,"
Because I know that they're just words
And your words are never true.

So here I come to an ending
I've ran out of things to say,
There's just one thing I forgot
I don't feel like loving you today.

*I love you, I love you not, I love you, Maybe.*
*Brandy Smith*

I have this chance
For my own fairy-tale ending
But I keep having second thoughts
On just how I feel
Could this be my
Happily ever after
Or is this
The beginning of a big disaster
I keep wishing
He's the one
But the sparks I use to feel
Have just gone numb
I still get butterflies
And chills up mine spine
But to me it's not enough
I want him to be mine
But as I search for him
I know he isn't around
Screaming inside my head
Yet never making a sound

You chase her
And end up getting hurt more,
I don't understand
What are you fighting for?

She's playing with your emotions
Cutting deeper every time,
I pick up the pieces time after time
Wishing you were mine

Can you tell that I can't breathe
Every time you are around
Forgetting everything important to me
To make sure you don't fall down

Risking it all for you
To give you what you think you need
You don't even notice
Everything you want is what we should be

Thoughts roll around
Inside my head
Making me think
Of what he said
Words so harsh
Spoken like a "true man"
But what happened to the "boy"
What happened to my friend?
Did he get lost
When we fell apart
Or was he never there
Right from the start
Promises that he broke
Rip me to shreds
Only three words he spoke
Filled my heart with dread

Can you feel the pain
You caused me,
All my wasted hours
Trying to be someone who isn't even close to me.

Can you see my fake smile
The one painted on my face,
All the memories we've had
I wish I could just erase.

Do you even care
About how I still feel for you,
Or was I just a waste of your time
Because you had nothing better to do.

Was it all a joke
Some funny game,
Did I mean anything to you
Or was I a person with no name?

Thoughts rush through my mind
Tearing at my soul
And wasting my time
Making me feel
Unless,
Worthless,
To you.
But I know that's a lie
You say I'm your everything
And that you'd do anything for me
But what do those words really mean
Am I really what you say I am
Am I really the world to you
These thoughts run through me
Making
Me
Confused.
I never gave you a second chance
Because I was afraid
I kept us apart
So now I sit here, so sad and alone
With a black hole instead of a heart

You gave me chance after chance
I ruined everyone
You said I destroyed you
And what I did can't be undone
But you don't understand
By tearing us apart
I destroyed myself too
And broke both our hearts
I know no matter
How many sorrys I say
All the pain I caused you
Won't just go away
But before you say
Those words so cruel
Hear me out
Listen once more to the words of a fool
I have never
F
A
L
L
E
N so hard,
For anyone but you
And I know you felt the same way
Remember, love doesn't walk away–people do,
And if we end today and go our separate ways
I don't want you to someday see,
You'll think back and say to yourself
"Wow that girl really did love me . . ."

You spoke so softly
Those lovely words of charm,
Never did I think
They would turn into words of harm.

Your striking smile
Your gorgeous face,
My own Heaven on Earth
If I could be anywhere
Your arms would be the place.

You never missed a beat
You always knew just what to say,
Such a smooth talker
You always got your way.

So when you told me
You wanted someone new,
My heart broke into pieces
Knowing there was nothing I could do.

Give me a reason
Not to move on,
Cause I've been waiting here
For far too long.

Dreaming about
You and me,
But my dreams aren't real
They're just fantasy.

So it's now or never
Because I'm not going to sit here
And wait forever

So don't waste my time
Better yet,
Do us both a favor
Don't be mine.

As I am sitting here
I look at both of you,
Thoughts rush through my head
I don't know what to do.

I guess I'm stupid
Because I don't know who to choose,
I like both of you
But who am I willing to lose.

I hide my feelings behind a smile
All I do is pretend,
My head hurts with thoughts of you
Will this pain ever end?

I'm lost in my thoughts
I set my standards to high,
I could say I don't love you
But that would be a lie.

I can't help but smile
When I look at you,
I hope you'll smile back
But you never do.

I'm seeing signs
That aren't really there,
I'm falling for you
But you'll never care.

For some reason
I know it's true,
That no matter how in love I am
I have no chance with you.

*I love you, I love you not, I love you, Maybe.*
*Brandy Smith*

Give me a reason to love you
I'm growing tired by the day,
I must not lose my temper
But I'm not going to walk away.

I know I shouldn't love you
Please help me just move on,
I'm tired of trying to keep strong
When everything goes wrong.

So tonight as I am crying
Don't bother to ask what's wrong,
I just want to forget you
I just want to move on.

Why do your harsh words
Cut me so deep,
You just walk away from
The empty promise you couldn't keep.

You turn your back on everything
I put my hope into,
And when I go to give you my heart
You walk away as if I mean nothing to you.

I was there when you were lost
And needed to be found,
But in my darkest hour
You were nowhere to around.

Invisible, in the again I felt
So quiet you could hear my heart break,
So blind even in the silence
You will never see your mistake.

.

You said we wouldn't work out
But we never really gave "us" a try,
I begged you not to leave
I discovered feelings love to lie.

Your memory wouldn't fade
I could never get away,
The more I wanted to run
The more your memory seemed to stay.

The moment you walked away
Echoed in my head,
I just wanted to forget
Yet I hung off every word you said.

All the butterflies and secrets
You promised you'd always be mine,
You promised to love me forever
But I guess forever was too long a time.

*I love you, I love you not, I love you, Maybe.*
*Brandy Smith*

The words came out in a whisper
My last silent plea,
I'm begging you to stay
But you just turn around and leave.

I don't understand what I did
For you to not even want to be my friend,
If I could show you how much your words hurt
You'd never be able to look me in the eyes again.

I can't keep chasing you around
For you to love me like you used to,
Suddenly I hate myself
For feeling everything I felt for you.

Tears fill my eyes
And agony fills my heart,
When you walked away
You left me alone and torn apart.

You say your heart hurts
Past the point of holding on,
You ask how you can stay
When everything is going wrong.

I give you a watery smile
Trying to hide what I really feel,
This can't be happening
This can't be real.

You looked relieved
Not to see any tears,
Just a heart break
A sound you didn't seem to hear.

I stand motion less
As you turn and walk away,
The tears began to form and fall
Because I can't make you stay.

My hearts shouting
Words my mouth couldn't say,
I whisper my truth
But if your feelings are gone
My words wouldn't have stopped you
Anyway.

A sweet poison
When love is gone,
You think it's for the best
But you are all wrong.

Excuses are made
In order to cover up the truth,
Lies always find their way out
Disguises are no use.

A slow massacre
Lingers in the distance,
A deadly suffering
If only by circumstance.

If twisted
Love can kill,
But no lies, just love
A wish can be fulfilled.

All the wonders love can bring
If embraced,
But to capture each of them
Love is one fear you must face.

All this time you've been in my head
I've been waiting and waiting
For the words you never said

We've started to drift apart
And you just don't seem to comprehend,
I can't keep trying my best
Just to lose over and over again.

On top of everything else
This is just too much,
I have to put my foot down
Because enough is enough.

I'm not saying I don't want you
Because I definitely do,
I'm just saying I can't do this anymore
I'm done chasing after you.

I had the right intentions
But I made one wrong turn,
It was my mistakes
And a hard lesson that had to be learned.

I feel so hard
And gave you my all,
I never would have guessed
You would just let me fall.

I thought our feelings ran down deep
Straight to the core,
But you turned away
And left me wanting more.

So now I'm left with nothing but memories
I'm lost and confused,
I never would have thought
You could make me feel so used.

My heart may be damaged
But it's still yours,
Even though I'm hurt
You're still the only one I'm fighting for.

*I love you, I love you not, I love you, Maybe.*
*Brandy Smith*

I tell you I love you
But you don't say it back,
I know you want out
But I don't want to face facts.

I try with all my power
To see the pain beneath your skin,
No matter how much I try and fight
I can't ever seem to win.

No other guy crosses my mind
Just let me in your heart
Just give me the time

Let's speak the truth
I'll give my all to you,
Just tell me I'm yours
Tell me you love me too.

My smile is gone
I'm past pretending I'm fine,
No longer in your heart
I'm just wishing you were mine.

I feel so hollow
Without you here,
I try to pull myself together
But I just break down in tears.

You picked me up
And helped me breathe,
But when my wall went down
You just turned around to leave.

The promises you made
I knew were to good to be true,
But I let myself believe them
And fell head over heels for you.

So now I sit here
Not knowing what to do,
I wish I could take back
Every word I said to you.

My heart is in pieces
And left on the floor,
Numbness has taken over
And I feel nothing anymore.

Dancing in the pouring rain
Not judging old and new,
My mind swirling all around
With blurred thoughts of you.

I'm cold and wet and all alone
Wondering where you are,
The tables are turned I'm at the edge
No longer in your arms.

The cold rain and hot tears
All began to mix,
I quickly began to fear
My pain cannot be fixed.

I tell myself to forget you
And go on with my life,
But memories of you flash in my mind
And keep me up at night.

Sometimes
I want to travel back in time,
Jump in jump out
I don't care as long as you're mine.

I know I meant something
And hopefully always will,
Because in the very end
Love never fails.

You took my hand
Told me you loved me more,
It seemed like forever passed
You were everything I was fighting for.

In the silence
Did you hear a shatter?
The broken promises
Only proved I didn't matter.

All this time
You just wanted me to disappear,
But even through the hurt
I'm still wishing you were here.

As you turned away
You didn't notice my heart break,
Or even the tears that streamed my face
When I realized I was your biggest mistake.

She's thinking of him
You can hear the smile in her voice,
Falling in love with him was beyond her control
She had no choice.

She bites her lips
And closes her eyes,
Just thinking of what he said
Gives her butterflies.

When her kisses her
The world fades away,
She won't admit it to herself
But she'd give anything to make him stay.

She gets jealous
When he looks at any other girls,
He has no idea
That he is her entire world.

So if I'm the girl
When will you finally see?
You're the guy
In my fantasies.

*I love you, I love you not, I love you, Maybe.*
*Brandy Smith*

The words come out in an undertone
My last hushed plea,
I'm begging you to stay
But you just turn around and leave.

I don't understand what I did
For you to not want to be my friend,
But if I could show you how much your words hurt me
You'd never be able to look me in the eyes again.

I can't keep chasing you around
For you to love me like you used too,
Suddenly I hate myself
For feeling everything I felt for you.

Tears fill my eyes
An ache fills my heart,
When you walked away
You left me along in the dark.

Tonight I cried one million tears
Because I love you so,
Tonight I cried one million tears
Because I have to go.

Today I cried no tears at all
For I know you'll miss me,
Today I cried no tears at all
For staying here would be a fantasy.

But now I cry a river
And let out a sigh,
But now I cry a river
Because I have to say goodbye.

I remember the look in your eyes
On that unforgettable night,
So hallow and cold
Now I know what "I don't love you" feels like.

If only I had known
But I was so unaware,
Mislead to believe
You would always be there.

Perhaps for an instant
We could spin back the hands of time,
Maybe one final moment
I could make you mine.

I'm so sick of living off false hopes
I can't do this anymore,
I'm no different than you
Break my heart for what breaks yours.

Lines in a poem
Words in a song,
Whispered sweet nothings
Once here now gone.

Mixed emotions
Tossed around,
Looking for an escape
Words in which she can drown.

To hear your voice
Yet know you're gone,
Makes her wish
For another song.

Blackened heart
Touched with grace,
These words speak
Letting her know he can be replaced.

Press play
And listen to more rhymes,
Maybe this will the tune
Maybe she'll get lost in it this time.

Words run together
The beat pluses within,
She'll play track after track
Just trying to forget him.

*I love you, I love you not, I love you, Maybe.*
*Brandy Smith*

Tears run down her face
She can't catch her breath,
She's waiting for him to stop her
But he hasn't realized she's serious yet.

She pleads her soon—to—be last words
Her only regret,
Not proving their meant to be
Her pleads go unmet.

He doesn't listen
He just turns away,
Pain sears her heart
She knows he has nothing left to say.

He gave up on her
She's trying not to give up on herself,
But how can she believe
When there's no one here to help.

Alone in this empty house
Listening to music on loud,
Eyes closed & pressed against the wall
Trying to drown the silence out.

My heart hurts
But it's nothing I can't take,
Compared to your sad eyes
I'll smile to the world, even if it's fake.

The music is pounding
The tempo running in my head,
I try to hear the lyrics
But I'm stuck off every word you said.

Chorus chimes in
And tears slide down my cheeks,
Wet and salty
But still in time with the songs beat.

On my knees
I feel weak,
Where I can't sing along
The music speaks.

*I love you, I love you not, I love you, Maybe.*
*Brandy Smith*


We're both at different ends
Fighting each other,
Ropo hold tightly our hands
Pulling against one another.

We want the same thing
But we both need a side,
Always a struggle
Always a wild ride.

You pull; I tug
In this unending war,
Fighting for each other
Who loves who more?

In this game no one wins
And no one's keeping score,
And during all the tugging
I forget what I'm fighting for.

Love me like the world is ending
& let's drop this rope,
We don't need to fight
We only need hope.

I'd stay up all night
For the chance to star in your dreams,
We'd make them into reality
And prove things aren't always how they seem.

I'd make you happy
Beyond anyone else,
And in your slumber
You'd be smiling to yourself.

But open your eyes
To the chaos of the world,
Take my hand; I'll lead you
I can be your girl.

The heartbeat of loneliness is loud
and it drives you mad,
In the stillness you remember
What you lost; what you truly had.

The pain runs deep
And tears pour,
You had everything you wanted
And so much more.

Keep your eyes closed
To the beauty of your dreams,
Everything is how you want it
But nothing is as it seems.

My mind is full
Of the little things I'll miss,
The sweet smell of rain
Or the sparks during a lasting kiss.

My eyes are dry
But my heart is too,
If only I could get rid of the feeling
Of meaning nothing to you.

Memories run through my mind
Over and over they play,
I did everything I could
In every single way.

A glance in the mirror
Makes me turn away in disgust,
I can feel the weight of disappointment
The loss of trust.

Always second best
Compared to everyone else,
Is this why I want to go?
Because I sicken myself?

The tears come slowly
Because now you're on my mind,
Your smile is what lingers
I wish I could press rewind.

*I love you, I love you not, I love you, Maybe.*
*Brandy Smith*

I'd tell you I love you again and again
And make my love known,
In your strong arms I'd stay
Because your arms feel like home.

Now we're at a close
A goodbye is here,
Remember that I love you
And in your heart I'll always be near.

*I love you, I love you not, I love you, Maybe.*
*Brandy Smith*

Sitting with you
Just being myself,
Whenever I'm with you
I don't have to be anyone else.

Your careless smile
Takes my breath away,
Your face is easy to read
Even when you have nothing to say.

You can always make me laugh
When everything is crashing down,
No matter how I feel
You can make my heart pound.

Looking pass imperfections
Wishing you could see the signs,
We may be the best of friends
But deep down I wish you were mine.

A glance in my direction
Shows the simple truth I can't deny,
And though it may hurt me
To you, I'll always be one of the guys.

# Misery

"I don't think of all the misery, but of all the beauty that still remains."

—Anne Frank

You tell me not to give up
And to stay strong,
But how can I when my world is crashing down
And everything has gone wrong.

I'm putting on my armor
Building up my shield,
I can't go to fight
If nothing is what I feel.

I'm searching for my reason
To know what I'm fighting for,
Along the way I lost my purpose
I have no fight left in me anymore.

I keep wishing and hoping
Someone will be there,
It seems to me
Hope never got anyone anywhere.

One last chance
To make some memories,
One last chance
To live in fantasy.

One more moment
To be best friends,
One more moment
With no goodbyes or the ends.

One more day
To have no regrets,
One more day
To remember how we met.

One more hello
Just to say goodbye,
One more hello
To live different lives.

One more promise
We will never keep,
One more promise
We will never meet.

One more dance
In your arms,
One more dance
To remind me why I'm holding on.

No one ever knows
What they have until it's gone,
You never realize it was everything
That kept you holding on.

But what happens if you knew
Disaster before it came,
It couldn't be stopped and you couldn't just walk away
Then where would your feelings aim?

Could you endure it?
With a smile on your face,
Or would the pain plainly show
Because it couldn't be erased.

Would you pretend to be happy?
Just so others wouldn't know,
The pain just under the surface
The pain you wouldn't show.

You can close your eyes to the things you don't want to see
But you can't close your heart to the things you don't
want to feel,
I'm trying not to think but reality and my dreams mix
And imagination begins to feel so real.

I close my eyes trying to shut everything out
But I can't seem to push these thoughts aside,
It all runs together as I'm drowning in the despair
And just adds to the tears I can't seem to hide.

I want to run away from my own thoughts
The ones I'm unable to forget,
My mind is taking over
And I'm caught in an internal battle I can't fight or forfeit.

Daughter, sister, best friend
With a secret to hide
Wild, enraged, and foolish
Dying from the inside

Mistaken, hurt and upset
Unsure what to do
Defies, strayed, just trying to survive
Disbelief for what she's turning herself into

Parties, drugs and such fun
No reason to say no
Buzzed, happy and numb
Just going with the flow

Cold, useless and empty
Watching everything fade and trickle together
Wounded, suffering and scared
Begging "please don't let this be forever"

Frightened, forgotten and alone
Wondering which way is out
Running, hiding and concealing
Uncertain what life is really about

Angry, discouraged and disappearing into a deep depression
Gone without a trace
Ran before, runs now, and will always be running
Death—something even she couldn't face

Remember the moments you can't put into words
They seem to go by so fast,
Smiles, love, and laughter
They all never seem to last.

Remember the things
That took it all away,
The hurt, pain, and sadness
The words you were never able to say.

All the broken wishes
All the crushed hopes and dreams,
Showing you the truth
Things are never as they seem.

I feel the urge
For that moment of pain,
Those few precious minutes
That would create weeks of shame.

I can't decide
If it's worth it,
Me hating myself
Just for a quick fix.

The numbness I crave
I know the pain won't last,
How can I want something
That's gone so fast?

Deep down I know it is wrong
And I shouldn't think this way,
But that doesn't clear my head
And make my thoughts go away.

Blade in hand
I trace the scars I've already caused,
But a shred of hope reaches the surface
And makes me pause.

Pieces of me lay broken all around
I hear people laughing
Yet there's no one here to make a sound
I feeling like screaming
Ripping apart
This feeling I have
Held heavy in my heart
I want to let go
Of everything I can't help but miss
I want to shine through
And have a chance at happiness
But as I sit here
Trying desperately to ease my pain
I only sink lower
Hiding my shame
I know things will change
Someday in due time
But what if someday isn't fast enough
Pulled two ways between my heart and my mind
I guess I have no choice
I'll have to wait and see
What will happen and who
Will take that chance on me

Tears streaked down her face
She had given up on herself,
There was no fight left in her
So how could she expect fight from
anyone else?

No one ever noticed
Her smile was fake,
No one ever cared enough
To try and help forget her mistakes.

She ripped open old scars
That never fully healed,
Brought back the past
And the secrets it concealed.

Alone and unheard
She pushed everyone away,
Never did she realize
The price she had to pay.

A cry for help
Echoed in the dark,
No one seemed to hear
The fear trying to escape her heart.

You act like I can't hear you
You act like I can't see,
I'm not as dumb as you think
I know you're talking about me.

So when I go confront you
You'll lie straight to my face,
Don't say you're sorry
Because those words you can't erase.

A promise unkept
Here comes an end,
A lie you told
Just shows you were never a true friend.

Time is running out
Moments passing by,
The life I thought I lived
Gone in the blink of an eye.

You never know what you have
Till it's gone,
And you're left
In the darkness all alone.

So live in the now
And live like it's your last today,
Because tomorrow's not promised
You never know if you're going to stay.

I never thought
It'd be so hard,
To lose a friend
Or fix a broken heart.

But when you try and pick up the pieces
Of your shattered life,
It only hurts you more
And takes away your will to fight.

You walk around
Pretending nothing is wrong,
But your heart aches with the hurting
And you're finding it hard to stay strong.

To blind to see a way out
From the pain you feel inside,
Pushing away people
From the emotions you're unable to hide.

You're left with a choice
The moment is here,
Either to dwell on the broken pieces
Or walk away forgetting your fear.

It's like looking from a distance
Standing in the background,
Watching everyone's life move forward
As mine is crashing down.

I can hide the truth behind my smile
But the fear is in my eyes,
I'm not ready to let go
I'm not ready for goodbyes.

I used to think time drug on
But it flies by when you're almost gone,

I have two choices
Either hide away and welcome death,
Or start living life to the fullest
Until my very last breath.

Life doesn't stop for anyone
Time won't pause because you want it to,
You must stop yourself
And think of what really matters to you.

Life flashes before your eyes
Memories, moments, mess ups and mistakes,
You end up breaking down
Because you can't put on the breaks.

Life goes on
And time heals all pain,
At least I know when I'm gone
My memory will remain.

*I love you, I love you not, I love you, Maybe.*
*Brandy Smith*

I never thought
It'd be so hard,
To lose a friend
Or fix a broken heart.

But when you try and pick up
The pieces of your splintered life,
It only hurts you more
And takes away your will to fight.

You walk around
Pretending nothing's wrong,
But your heart aches with the hurting
And you're finding it hard to stay strong.

To blind to see a way out
From the pain you feel inside,
Pushing people away from the emotions
You're trying so hard to hide.

*I love you, I love you not, I love you, Maybe.*
*Brandy Smith*

There's a distance in her eyes
That no one seems to see,
In her mind she's thinking
Her only escape may be deadly.

She goes home
Only to be hurt worse,
She hides her shame
Her secret, her curse.

Others see
But they don't ask,
She disguises it well
All behind a vacant mask.

She never says a word
Never cries out for help,
An empty shell she's come to be
Not even knowing herself.

No one worries
They don't bother to show they care,
Until the day
She's no longer there.

*I love you, I love you not, I love you, Maybe.*
*Brandy Smith*


Under the covers
I don't make a sound,
Maybe he won't come in tonight
The floor creaks; hope has let me down.


I hear him shuffle
Down the hall,
Maybe he won't stop at my door
Still, I push myself closer to the wall.


He comes in
I pray he can't hear my heart beat,
Tonight must be another night
When God just doesn't hear me.


His weight forces the air out of me
I'm too scared to try and turn away,
This is just one of his games
And I have no choice but to play.

*I love you, I love you not, I love you, Maybe.*
*Brandy Smith*

He fumbles for a moment
Frustration crosses his face,
Time goes in slow motion as he takes
Something that can't be replaced.

He finishes and leaves
The same way he came in,
But its small relief
I know tomorrow it will happen again.

"Lord I'd do anything,
To keep him from walking back through
that door,"
Tears flow out
I know I can't do this anymore.

Shutting down
Trying to go numb,
But the memories keep attacking
And in my mind I have nowhere to run.

The tears just keep coming
I can't find control over myself,
Searching for my answer
Only to find I've turned into someone else.

Unable to fake enough emotion
Just to pretend,
I know in the long run you will deny me
And leave me with no one to help defend.

I can't put on a fake smile
Much less one that's real,
I wish I could beg for help
But for that I'd have to want to feel.

It hurts so much
To think of the way things are,
I never thought I could feel this way
I never thought life would be so hard.

My hand wraps around your fingers
And I'm tugging you along,
Anywhere, everywhere, across the universe
At four years old, mommy can do no wrong.

Tea time, dolls, and dress up
My mom's my one and only playmate,
I can't wait be just like her
Mommy, my best friend at eight.

Bed without dinner because I was bad
Mommy is so mean,
I can't wait till I grow up
I hate mommy at thirteen.

Broken-hearted and crushed
That boy made me feel like a queen,
Torn up, in tears, and in mommy's arms
Mommy can fix me at sixteen.

I have all the answers
Independent, self-assured, and free,
The world is mine to take
Mommy is just a memory at twenty-three.

Running around—work, kids, and him
There's always so much to do,
So caught up in my own life
Mommy is invisible at thirty-two.

Life is fast, and I'm searching for understanding
Now is when I turn to you,
Wise beyond your years
Mommy is my helper at forty—two.

My hands are sturdy compared to yours
And you need me more each day,
I try to remember a time when I needed you
At fifty—six, mommy is starting to wilt away.

Your hair is white and your laugh lines big
I hope I get the trait,
Bright and cheerful as ever
Mommy is my everything at sixty—eight.

(continued)

I wish you were here to help me with my struggles
My heart is with you in Heaven,
So many wasted years have passed because of me
Mommy is gone at seventy-seven.

I'm just like you—exactly what I always wanted
And I'll soon be by your side,
The road is coming to a close, but the secret of life was found
Mommy and I will be together once again at eighty-five.

*I love you, I love you not, I love you, Maybe.*
*Brandy Smith*


I can feel you pushing away
And shutting down,
Everything is so strained
Like life and our choices hasn't made its way around.


We're at a fork in the road
And I see the end could be near,
Yet even in the heartbreak
I still wish I had someone here.


Let's not drag this out
If it's done for,
Let's not pretend if neither of us
Can do it anymore.


Slower smaller steps
Is what I need,
You may hate it
But it's the way it's got to be.


I'm off the cliff
No longer on the edge,
Not hanging on by much
But at least not hanging on by a thread.


Too much to fast will make me run
And you know this to be true,
But hopefully this time you can understand
Because the friend I need is you.


137

I thought this would be fun
Moving in with you,
My bool fi lend for years
We could be like sisters too.

We'd be together 24/7
And nothing would break us apart,
I guess neither of us seen this coming
Neither of us was that smart.

The yelling and ignoring
Grew at an alarming rate,
Every "make-up" never lasted
And it was our friendship I was beginning to hate.

I don't know how to fix
This mess I've put us through,
I've already lost so much
I don't want to lose a best friend too.

Leaving is the only solution I can think of
Because we fight more than we're friends,
And if something doesn't change fast
Our friendships going to end.

Over and over again
These fights carry on,
I see no end to them
And think maybe I'm just better off gone.

The rumors spread
And the whispers fly,
I hear what you really think of me
And in our friendship I see nothing but lies.

I confront you
Seeking out the truth,
But another lie is told to cover up
And I know my efforts are no use.

I sit here in vain
Still unsure how to proceed,
You pushed me too far
But your friendship is like an acute need.

Thank you and I'm sorry
Is all that's left to say?
I have nothing of real value to give
And to you that's not okay.

I wish my friendship was enough
To keep us from this,
A goodbye is in order
A friendship I'll surely miss.

*I love you, I love you not, I love you, Maybe.*
*Brandy Smith*

My world is crashing down
No time to catch my breath,
The walls ure closing in
Soon there will be nothing left.

My head is screaming
Telling me to run away,
But something in my heart holds me back
Begging me to stay.

Hollow hearts
Empty eyes,
A world with a fake image of perfection
A warm heart filled with lies.

How can I get up
When everything had gone so wrong,
How can I keep trying
When this has been going on for so long.

My hope is fading
I don't know how to believe,
Every time I let someone in my heart
They always turn around and leave.

# Affection

"Love is your favorite food for breakfast, lunch, and dinner."

—Bo Burnham

Don't be afraid
I'm never going to leave you,
This is beyond happy
Just say that you want to be with me too.

You flash me a deadly smile
And make me forget how to breathe,
Don't walk away please
Promise you'll fight for me.

I see you and the background blurs
I need you closer,
You're what I want
I don't need time to think it over.

Love is about facing your biggest fears
So always do what you're afraid to do,
Jump a fall hard
Because I'm here to catch you.

*I love you, I love you not, I love you, Maybe.*
*Brandy Smith*

I don't know what's happening
I can't find the words to say,
How I feel when I'm around you
I just can't explain.

Whenever you come near me
I feel myself begin to blush,
I want to hold for just a few moments longer
Every time we touch.

Your presence is so overpowering
Your smile weakens my knees,
Just the thought of your lips on mine
Makes it hard for me to breathe.

Do you share my feelings?
Has forever finally begun,
Questions eat away at me
And make me wonder if you think I am the one.

You accept me warmly just the way I am
I love that you see me like no one else can,
I love you like no one has before
I can love you forever and still crave more.

You put the smile in my voice
The sparkle in my eyes,
You only have to look at me
To give me butterflies.

When I'm without
No other sound appears,
My heart is the only sound
That's pounding in my ears.

You make the pain go away
You make my broken heart fade,
I can't be without you
You're like an addiction that I crave.

I can't believe this feeling
It must be a crime,
The way I stole your heart
The way you stole mine.

You look my way
Our eyes meet,
My heart flutters
And skips a beat.

I don't understand
The way my heart is contenting,
But I can't help myself
You're my happy ending.

I need you so much closer
Don't let me forget,
The way we feel for each other
It will be our best-kept secret.

I'm telling myself
Just to breathe,
But I know in the end
People always leave.

I was yours to have
But you; an endless chase,
Still the love I felt for you
Can never be replaced.

I tried to change
Our nightmares into dreams,
But nothing broke the silence
And I surrounded myself with empty screams.

Now I'm gasping for air
Remembering everything you swore,
You promised but I knew
I have always loved you more.

When I look in your eyes
The world disappears,
I forget all my worries
Problems and fears.

You're my breath of air
My light of day,
When my words cluster up
You seem to always understand what I say.

You're my everything
And all that's in-between,
When I look in your eyes
It's the greatest sight I've ever seen.

Falling in love is said to be the best way
to kill your heart
Because then it isn't yours anymore,
But I'd gladly rip mine apart
As long as it's yours.

*I love you, I love you not, I love you, Maybe.*
*Brandy Smith*

I love to see you smile
The sparkle in your eye,
Everything about you
You are the perfect guy.

I told you how I felt before
My heart ended up,
Being ripped out
And left to die on the floor.

I shortly came to realize
Your friendship was enough,
I'm still loving you forever
If only my love was enough.

I smile because you smile
I cry because you cry,
I'm happy that you love her
For reasons I don't know why.

So when you lie awake at night
Just think of what I said,
I know you will realize
I love you as a friend.

*I love you, I love you not, I love you, Maybe.*
*Brandy Smith*

My world stopped
The minute I called
I didn't talk much
But I heard your sweet voice
I can't wait for the future
It's so far away
I know I'll be with you one day
But until then
I sit here waiting for a sign
I feel as if I'm wasting my time
Do you have a place
For me in your heart
A place where love stands still
And love is all we will ever feel

You and me forever
Love knows no bounds,
My knees are getting weak
In the silence my heart pounds.

Speaking straight to my heart
Simply by looking in my eyes,
Love never fails
We just have to try.

We can last the distance
No matter how far apart,
It's just a test of our love
And you're still holding onto my heart.

My cheeks hurt from smiling
And butterflies never felt so good,
If we cold run away and never look back
We both know we would.

Everyone has a weakness
And you happen to be mine,
Scared to death of letting you inside
But for you; I'll put it all on the line.

Take my hand
And I know I'll be okay,
When you proudly declare
"I'll be in love with you forever and always."

Looking from a distance
Standing from afar,
I don't care what happens
As long as I am wherever you are.

Time is flying by
And I'm begging it to slow down,
My pleads go unanswered
The silence begins to grow and surround.

I see your smile
And I know I'll be okay,
I'll push it all aside
And in your arms I'll stay.

You're like my cure
For all things unfair,
With you I can smile
Even though I'm scared.

So pull me close
And kiss me like you mean it,
Whisper those sweet words
And make me forget.

You tell me I'm your soldier
Fighting this war,
Sometimes I wish I could forfeit
Because I don't think I can fight anymore.

I've put in blood, sweat, and tears
And trying my very best,
But it's getting harder and harder to fight
When I'm aching for a rest.

I just want you to hold me in your arms
And tell me everything will be alright,
Murmur that you love me
And that we will win this fight.

I can conquer the world with one hand
If you're holding the other,
We will get through this battle
One foot after another.

Promise me you will stay
Swear you won't give up on me,
With you by my side
I can do anything.

*I love you, I love you not, I love you, Maybe.*
*Brandy Smith*


I don't need a title
To know that I'm yours,
This feeling inside
Is difficult to ignore.

Your smile
Is all I need to see,
To make me happy
For all of eternity.

Perhaps I let myself go overboard
In falling so hard for you,
Please try and understand
And don't misconstrue.

My heart is here
For you to take,
This is beyond words
And you just can't fight fate.

Whisper that you love me
Make my heart skip a beat,
Then stop time; go back
Let's put it on repeat.

Look me in the eyes
And promise you'll stay,
Swear that you love me
Forever and always.

I don't know what is happening
I can't find the words to say,
How I feel when I'm around you
I just can't explain.

Whenever you come near
I feel myself began to blush,
I want to hold you for just a few moments longer
Every time we touch.

You presence is so overpowering
You smile weakens my knees,
And just the thought of your lips on mine
Make its hard for me to breathe.

Do you share my feelings?
Has forever finally begun,
The questions eat away at me
And make me wonder if you think I'm the one.

You accept me warmly
Just the way I am,
I love that you can see me
Like no one has before.

When I look in your eyes
The world disappears,
I forget my worries, problems
Stresses and all my fears.

You my breath of air
My light of day,
And when my words cluster up
You always seem to understand what I say.

You give me a reason
To wake up tomorrow and the next,
You easily make my day
With something as little as a text.

When the phone rings I answer
Hoping it is you,
When I stumble your arms are always open
For me to run into.

You're my everything
And all that's in-between,
When I look into your eyes
It's the greatest sight I've ever seen.

Falling in love is said to be
The best way to kill your heart,
Because it's not yours anymore
But I'd gladly rip mine apart
As long as I'm yours.

Sometimes you have to pretend to be okay
Hold back the tears,
And walk away
From all the hurt and pain.

Remember the memories
Hold them close to your heart,
Babe this feeling isn't make believe
Please don't let us fall apart.

You can handle me at my worst
Gave me wings an taught me how to fly,
You were there when I needed you most
I see the best of me in your eyes.

But if this is what you want
Then we will say our goodbyes,
I'm willing to risk everything for you to stay
But if you won't at least the Lord knows I tried.

You can run as far as you need
But in the end I'll still be right here,
Waiting for you to come back
And face your fears.

Stare at me
Like I'm your world,
Pull me close and whisper
Those three beautiful words.

Tell me I'm gorgeous
And that you never want to let me go,
Scream me a love song
So that the whole world will know.

I don't need fame or gold
Or even Mr. Right,
"I love you" is all I need
To stay in the fight.

Every time I see you
I catch my breath and get butterflies,
With feelings so strong
We'll never say goodbye.

Just one look
And she knew,
No clue who he was
Or what she was getting herself into,

She held beauty
Anyone with eyes could see,
He couldn't help thinking
"That's the girl for me."

Time runs slow and fast
A beautiful mess,
Pulling together two different hearts
Leaving them breathless.

Falling hard
Falling fast,
Falling in love
Falling for the hope it could last.

Counting on him with every step
Like the air for her survival,
The kind of head over heels love
You could see in her smile.

She was his world
Every move she made kept him memorized,
The deep kind of love
You could see in his eyes.

Grab my hand
Pull me close,
Whisper secrets to me
That no one else knows.

Look at me
Like I'm your world,
Point me out in a crowd and say
"That's my girl."

Take me as I am
With all my mess ups and mistakes,
Show me you love me
Whatever it takes.

Pick me up and spin me around
Trying to show off and be strong,
We'll make this work
Let's prove everyone wrong.

Tell me your hopes and dreams
Let me in your heart,
Be my light and I'll be yours
Help me through the dark.

Flash my smile
Stop my heart,
We'll run away if we have to
And never grow apart.

Stare at me
With your deep eyes,
Look at my soul
And give me butterflies.

Tell me you love me
More and more every day,
Promise me
It will always be this way.

Make me laugh
Drive me insane,
No matter what happens
Vow that love will always remain.

I can hear your heart beat
It's the soundtrack of my life,
Wrapping all around me
Holding me tight.

I wished I knew
What you were thinking,
When you flash a smile my way
My heart is racing at the words you didn't even say.

When you smile
Your eyes light up a room,
It hits me every time
Like a sonic boom.

I'm reaching for you
If you are reaching for me,
What if our love makes us into
What we were meant to be.

When I wanted to give up
You taught me how to fight,
Now Ihoughts of you spin all around
And keep me up at night.

We've been through hell and back
We've only just begun,
Here is our moment to take the chance
There's no need to run.

I'll take your heart
If you take mine and hold it till the end,
Don't worry about "what ifs"
We have a lifetime to spend.

Take my hand
Don't be scared,
For no other girl will ever care about you
As much as I care.

Believe the words I speak
Because I have never been so sincere,
Weather we are lovers or fighters
I'll always be here

# Saved

"For it is by grace you have been saved, through faith—and this is not from yourselves, it is the gift of God-"

—Ephesians 2:8 (INV)

You never intended
For life to end up this way,
The chains that hold you
Are the chains that you have made.

You wake up to realize
You're on the verge of goodbye,
And your standard of living
Somehow got stuck on survive.

Each day is harder,
Harder than the last,
Drowning in your hurt
You're too caught up in your past.

Barely able to stand
You're dragging your feet,
Ready to fall on your knees
Lost in your own defeat.

Cries aching in your chest
Worthless, hopeless, and alone
Sinking farther
With no place to call home.

Don't you know you are loved?
You are forgiven from your sins,
Don't you know you are priceless?
You are more to Him.

Everyone says
To believe in Him,
That He'll love me
And forgive my sins.

Everyone says
He'll make everything right,
Help me with my problems
And put my worries out of sight.

Everyone says
That He is the best,
Let God guide you
And He will do the rest.

But no one sees
Inside me the war going on,
I fear even God can't change
All the things I've done wrong.

Light as feathers
Across rough skin,
As real as the ache in cheeks
During a lopsided grin,
God is working,
Even when you can't feel Him.

A glimmer in a lover's eyes
A stomach in a backspin,
The sunset over the city
A number on a napkin,
God is moving,
Even when you can't see Him.

Peace that consumes while lying on a chest
And listening to the heartbeat within,
The sound of a tear drop when a heart breaks
A beg for mercy after committing a sin,
God is healing,
Even when you can't hear Him.

Little girl
Fighting with all her might,
Caught in a never-ending storm
Keeps her from the light.

Screaming to the skies
Why does this always happen to her?
As tears stream from her eyes
She has nowhere to run too.

Warmth wraps around her
Giving her the hope she needs,
Draining out the misery
And helping her believe.

She stands up
Hands held high,
Thanking God for his mercy
His love is her battle cry.

His screams are thunderous through the door
And the rain is sliding down her cheeks,
Lightening has struck her heart
And the shadows on her skin will linger for weeks.

From her standpoint the storm is endless
Rolling on, leaving her spirit grim,
Exhausted of being wet
She runs from her house, her life, and him.

Out the door and into the night
Her feet carry her away,
Through the hurt, the ache, and the pain
Numb, she stumbles and her feet betray.

On her knees she is weak
Lost to the world,
But warmth steals the storm
And the darkness swirls.

Suddenly blighting light and she begins to understand
What it means to be brave,
Wrapped in God's eternal love
She is forever saved.

Pity Party Salvation—Part One

Everyone's loving life
As mine is tumbling down,
Wondering why their lives seem so perfect
As I take a look around.

Smiling faces and laughter
Ringing in my ears,
Only reminds me how alone I feel
I question if God can hear.

Why am I fighting so hard
When everyone else has it easy,
Why am I struggling so much
This isn't how it should be.

God is whom I blame
And rage consumes me,
"*My Child*" He whispers,
"You don't need your eyes to see."

I don't understand
Which only makes things worse,
Where is God when I need Him
This loneliness only hurts.

Pity Party Salvation—Part Two

I scream to the sky
It echoes in the night,
On my knees I hear Him
*"Live by Faith and not by sight."*

*"You are not alone*
*I'm by your side,*
*I know everything about you*
*Even the things you try so hard to hide,"*

*"You are not alone*
*I promise you My Child,*
*On your darkest days*
*I strive to see your smile,"*

*"Though others may seem happy*
*It is merely just a face,*
*Worldly things do not fill the hole*
*Inside your heart where I have a place,"*

*"Although it is tough*
*And seems like I'm not there,*
*I am always beside you*
*Trying to show how much I care,"*

*"the world is a wicked place*
*Full of destruction and lies,*
*But you are whole through Me*
*You are an angel in my eyes."*

Now is the time
We come together in your name,
Heal our hearts, Lord
Take away our shame.

All material things
Useless, compared to You,
You are the One and the Only
You are the Real Truth.

So as we come together
Anywhere is the place,
You are what we come for
To draw nearer to Your breathtaking face.

Your holy embrace
Fills us to the brim,
Sharing Your knowledge with others
Unable to hold the beauty in.

Come Lord,
We want so much more of You,
Only You can do everything
Only You can make us new.

These burdened chains hold me back
Reminding me of my failures and mistakes,
Dragging myself on the ground in order to budge
Heavy with iron, guilt, and ache.

Through the pain I grow strong
Muscles began to move,
I feel the sting but I can think around it
Knowing in the end I have nothing to lose.

Compared to His weight mine is light
And my burdens pale,
He took on every sin and won
Yet here I am oppressed with another fail.

How can I be angry
When He has already won the fight,
How can I be so foolish
When in His arms I know everything will be alright.

*I love you, I love you not, I love you, Maybe.*
*Brandy Smith*

On that cross I lay
Bearing every sin,
Just so I could save you
And carry you in.

Every word that was spoken
Was nothing but the truth,
If you won't believe them
What else can I do?

You try to pretend
And say there's nothing wrong,
Sweet child I created you
I know when you're struggling to stay strong.

Let me wrap my arms around you
And bring you a better day,
No matter what I'll still love you
More than words could ever say.

No matter what I'll still love you
And hope to be,
In your heart
I hope to be

Stars, tears, and air
You made everything,
I'm only one soul, one life
Are you someone who I can let my heart cling?

Heaven, the cosmos, and gravity
All that's in between,
With that vast distance
How much could I really mean?

Under the weight of my shame
When I doubt and am unable to feel,
Are you by my side?
Are you real?

Is your love underneath
Every aching scar?
Could you heal this breaking
And hold onto my heart?

There's a girl in that church pew
Singing all those rehearsed lines,
Listening to the preacher
Telling her to let her light shine.

All she's thinking is
She's stumbled too much to be loved,
Failed to many times before
To not be misjudged.

She will do better
Or so she tries to believe,
In her mind her strength is too feeble
For this goal to be achieved.

Though this verse she has overlooked
By His stripes she is healed,
Through her brokenness
Her true purpose has been revealed.

Letting go isn't easy
Even with no reason to hold on,
How much courage would it take
To be more than halfway gone?

Love is in the breaking
Of a sad heart,
Unable to get past the past
Of a beautiful flower pulled apart.

Love is near
The lonely soul,
Trying to grip the things
That once made them whole.

Love is here
Pouring from His hands,
Love is soon
In the footing of His plans.

Love is the Lord
Full of mercy, forgiveness, and grace,
Lord is the Lord
Craving for your sweet embrace.

# About the Author

Brandy Smith is a budding author who writes based on her experiences. She is a college freshman pursuing a degree in English. When she is not writing books or reading them, Brandy is an artist, and leads a life for God. Born in Aurora, Colorado she now resides in Amarillo, Texas. You can contact her at brandy_smith19@yahoo.com.